W9-BNG-273

TOP 10
SPORTS
★STARS★

FOOTBALL'S TOP 10 QUARTERBACKS

Barry Wilner

Enslow Publishers, Inc.
40 Industrial Road
Box 398
Berkeley Heights, NJ 07922
USA
http://www.enslow.com

Library of Congress Cataloging-in-Publication Data

Wilner, Barry.
  Football's top 10 quarterbacks / Barry Wilner.
      p. cm. — (Top 10 sports stars)
  Includes bibliographical references and index.
  Summary: "A collective biography of the top 10 quarterbacks, both past and present, which includes accounts of game action, career statistics, and more"—Provided by publisher.
  ISBN 978-0-7660-3469-3
  1. Quarterbacks (Football)—United States—Biography—Juvenile literature. 2. Quarterbacks (Football)—Rating of—United States—Juvenile literature. I. Title.
  GV939.A1W58 2010
  796.3320922—dc22
  [B]
                            2009027175

Printed in the United States of America

052011 Lake Book Manufacturing, Inc., Melrose Park, IL

10 9 8 7 6 5 4 3 2

To Our Readers: We have done our best to make sure all Internet Addresses in this book were active and appropriate when we went to press. However, the author and the publisher have no control over and assume no liability for the material available on those Internet sites or on other Web sites they may link to. Any comments or suggestions can be sent by e-mail to comments@enslow.com or to the address on the back cover.

♻ Enslow Publishers, Inc., is committed to printing our books on recycled paper. The paper in every book contains 10% to 30% post-consumer waste (PCW). The cover board on the outside of each book contains 100% PCW. Our goal is to do our part to help young people and the environment too!

Illustration Credits: All images courtesy of the Associated Press/Wide World Photos, except p. 42, courtesy of the Everett Collection, Inc.

Cover Illustration: Associated Press/Wide World Photos.

TOP
10

CONTENTS

No sport is more of a team game than football, where eleven players working together is a must for success. Yet the guy in charge of it all on offense usually is the key to winning games—and, eventually, winning championships.

The ten star passers here all played for or won championships, some of them winning many times. Otto Graham, considered by some the father of all modern passers, took ten titles of some sort in two leagues, the All-American Football Conference (AAFC) and the National Football League (NFL). Terry Bradshaw and Joe Montana won four Super Bowls each, and no one would argue that their teams could have still been champs without them.

Montana was the man who made the West Coast Offense go for the San Francisco 49ers, and that offense became the style of choice in the 1980s and 1990s, and still flourishes in the NFL today. He also was the master of the comeback win, but no more so than John Elway, Dan Marino, or Tom Brady, who have been almost unstoppable in two-minute drills.

When the Baltimore Colts beat the New York Giants for the 1958 championship, still considered the greatest game ever played, it was the cool and calm of John Unitas, as much as his strong arm and accurate throws, that got the credit. Indeed, the term "field general," often used to describe QBs, probably was penned for Unitas.

But even before Johnny U and Graham, there was Sammy Baugh, perhaps the best all-around athlete ever to play the position. Baugh led the NFL in passing, punting, and intercepting passes as a two-way player in 1943.

There has been a straight line of great quarterbacks from Baugh's days until now, when Manning and Tom Brady, who won three Super Bowls in four seasons early in his career, have dominated. And all of them were dependable: Favre holds the record for consecutive starts for a non-kicker. Manning may someday break that.

No matter who holds what records, these are the best passers football has ever seen.

SAMMY BAUGH

SAMMY
BAUGH

Slingin' Sammy was his nickname, and for good reason. In his time, Sammy Baugh threw the ball like no one else.

He could also kick it better than anybody, and he played some tough defense, too. Yes, one of the greatest quarterbacks ever also was a terrific defensive back for the Washington

player growing up," said Baugh, who played shortstop and third base. "I thought I was going to be a big-league baseball player."[1]

Instead, he led TCU to a 29–7–3 mark, including victories in the Sugar and Cotton Bowls. While in college, he played in a wide-open offense that no professional teams used. So when Baugh joined the Redskins in 1937, slingin' wasn't in fashion. Running the ball was.

Sammy changed that, setting an NFL record in his first season with 81 completions for 1,127 yards. From there, Baugh got better, leading the league in passing six times, throwing for 187 touchdowns and, in 1945, completing an amazing 70.3 percent of his throws. This was a record that stood for thirty-five years.

And that wasn't all. Unlike more modern quarterbacks, Baugh played on offense and defense. In 1943, he led the NFL in passing, interceptions, and punting. In 1940, Baugh averaged 51.4 yards per punt. Baugh also played his entire career in the days when many players didn't wear face masks.

"There was one game where Sam threw four touchdown passes and intercepted four passes. Imagine that," said Don Maynard, one of football's top receivers, who was once coached by Baugh. "There's nobody any better than Sam Baugh was in pro football."[2]

That's why Baugh's No. 33 is the only number officially retired by the Redskins, and why Baugh was one of seventeen members of the very first class to enter the Pro Football Hall of Fame, in 1963.

The Redskins won two championships and made the NFL title game five times in Baugh's sixteen seasons with them. In 1994, Baugh made the NFL's 75th anniversary team, one of four quarterbacks selected—along with Otto Graham, Johnny Unitas, and Joe Montana.

As a measure of how great a player Baugh was, the award given to the best college quarterback each year by the Touchdown Club of Columbus (Ohio) is named the Sammy Baugh Trophy.

SAMMY BAUGH

BORN: March 17, 1914, Temple, Texas.

. . . .

HIGH SCHOOL: Temple High School; Sweetwater High School, Texas.

. . . .

COLLEGE: Texas Christian University.

. . . .

PRO CAREER: Washington Redskins, 1937–1952.

. . . .

RECORDS: NFL passing, punting, and interception leader in 1943.

. . . .

HONORS: Pro Football Hall of Fame (1963); Six-time NFL passing leader.

. . . .

TERRY BRADSHAW

TERRY
BRADSHAW

To many of today's football fans, Terry Bradshaw is the guy who clowns around on a TV
pregame show. To Steelers fans, he's only the
greatest quarterback in Pittsburgh history.

The Steel City loves its football, and the guys
who made Pittsburgh the city of champions
in the 1970s are special heroes. Bradshaw, the
top overall pick in the 1970 draft—the Steelers had never won a title at that time—was
the engineer of Pittsburgh's dynasty during
that decade.

Not only did Bradshaw throw the most
famous pass in NFL history—which Franco

Harris caught for the "Immaculate Reception" touchdown in a 1972 playoff game against Oakland—but he went on to guide the Steelers to four Super Bowl wins in seven seasons. And he did it at a time when the NFL was filled with future Hall-of-Fame quarterbacks.

"I loved winning. I didn't care. I just wanted to win," said Bradshaw, the first quarterback to win four Super Bowls. "I'd like people to say nothing else but: 'That sucker just loved to win.' That would cover it pretty good."[1]

Bradshaw was more than pretty good. The 1978 league Most Valuable Player as well as the MVP of the 1979 and 1980 Super Bowls, he had a powerful arm, strong body, and a sense of how to avoid pass rushers. He was a true team player, something Bradshaw learned growing up in Louisiana, where he set a national high school record for throwing the javelin. When he entered the Hall of Fame, Bradshaw immediately credited others, not himself.

"What does all of this mean? It means I was one of the best who ever played? No," he said. "What it means is that in football you don't get anything you don't share with people."[2]

Bradshaw was a savvy quarterback. He called his own plays for nearly his entire fourteen-season career, in which he threw for 27,989 yards and 212 touchdowns on a team with a run-first approach.

In the playoffs, he was even more dangerous.

"I studied the [thinking of] quarterbacks," said Cliff Harris, a four-time Pro Bowl safety for the Cowboys.

"I would look at the play: Why is Bradshaw running the play at this time? I'd look at Bradshaw. I could not figure out who he was keying. There was a frustration, because you might technically carry out a defense as best you could, but he could still beat you."[3]

TERRY BRADSHAW

BORN: September 2, 1948, Shreveport, Louisiana.

HIGH SCHOOL: Woodlawn High School, Shreveport, Louisiana.

COLLEGE: Louisiana Tech.

PRO CAREER: Pittsburgh Steelers, 1970–1983.

RECORDS: Super Bowl Touchdown Passes (9), Yards Passing (932); Playoff Touchdown Passes (30), Yards Passing (3,833).

HONORS: Pro Football Hall of Fame (1989); NFL Most Valuable Player (1978); Most Valuable Player, Super Bowls XII, XIV.

TOM BRADY

TOM
BRADY

For anyone who believes a great
quarterback can only be found near
the top of the draft, we present
Tom Brady.

For those who think only college superstars
make it big as NFL quarterbacks, we present
Tom Brady.

Brady went from a sometime-starter at
Michigan and a sixth-round draft pick to one
of the most successful QBs in NFL history. In
his first four seasons as a starter, Brady won
three championships. During the 2007 season,
in which the Patriots won every game until

losing to the Giants in the Super Bowl, "Tom Terrific" set a record with 50 touchdown passes and New England scored 589 points—more than any team in history. He was the league's most valuable player, too.

"To be honest, I'm surprised it took so long for him to get this recognition because he's sort of been our MVP since he stepped on the field in '01, in my mind," Patriots owner Robert Kraft said.[1]

"Individual awards haven't been as important to me as the team goals," Brady said. "While I'm very flattered to be honored [as MVP], my greatest satisfaction comes from winning games."[2]

Brady didn't look like a serious candidate to become such a brilliant pro when he left college as the 199th pick in the 2000 draft. He barely played as a rookie, throwing three passes, and wouldn't have gotten on the field in 2001 had starter Drew Bledsoe not gotten injured.

When Bledsoe went out in Game 2 that season, Brady took over—and started winning. And winning. He guided the Patriots into the playoffs and in his first Super Bowl, carried them past the heavily favored St. Louis Rams, earning MVP honors in a 20–17 win.

In both 2003 and 2004, New England went 14–2 and won the title, with Brady again being chosen Super Bowl MVP in a 32–29 victory against Carolina following the '03 season.

"The guy is just a winner, and I think he'll be a winner no matter what he does," said teammate Troy Brown, one of Brady's favorite receivers.[3]

As much as being a winner, Brady wants to be known as a good example to youngsters. "You look at Joe Montana, who was one of my role models growing up, Lance Armstrong . . ." he said. "They're all great role models for children and adults. . . . It's flattering to be mentioned in their company."[4]

TOM BRADY

BORN: August 3, 1977, San Mateo, California.

HIGH SCHOOL: Junipero Serra High School, San Mateo, California.

COLLEGE: University of Michigan.

PRO CAREER: New England Patriots, 2000–present.

RECORDS: Super Bowl Most Career Completions (100) and Game Completions (32); Most Regular Season Touchdown Passes (50).

HONORS: NFL Most Valuable Player (2007); Most Valuable Player, Super Bowls XXXVI, XXXIX.

JOHN ELWAY

JOHN
ELWAY

John Elway, one of the most talented quarterbacks in NFL history and the face of the Denver Broncos franchise, was once labeled a loser.

Elway had taken the Broncos to three Super Bowls in four years (1986, '87 and '89). When they got there, they were routed, and Elway had not played well in those title games. So people began saying he couldn't win the big one.

Then, from 1990 to 1996, the quarterback who could wing the ball 70 yards downfield or scramble away for long running gains couldn't get Denver back to the Super Bowl. In '96, the Broncos were the AFC's best team, but lost in their first playoff game to Jacksonville, then a second-year franchise.

"If you ask about frustrating times, that had to be up there," Elway said. "But I think it made us even more focused on being successful, and look what happened."[1]

What happened the next year was the Broncos, a wild-card team, getting back to the Super Bowl—and winning it.

The most memorable play of that victory over the defending champion Packers was Elway's scramble on which he was hit and spun completely around in midair. The play was nicknamed "Elway's Helicopter."

After finally winning a Super Bowl at age thirty-seven, the oldest quarterback to do so, Elway no longer heard the "loser" label.

"They made this game for quarterbacks, and you've got to win this game to be up there with the elite," he said. "It wouldn't have been a complete career [without a Super Bowl win]."[2]

For good measure, he led the Broncos to another championship the next season, then retired on top.

"Sometimes there is a player that becomes so important to us and so much our hero that his number and name become part of us," Denver owner Pat Bowlen said. "There will never be another No. 7 on the Broncos."[3]

Elway wasn't drafted by Denver. The Baltimore Colts took him as the first overall pick out of Stanford, but almost immediately traded him to the Broncos.

In Denver, Elway won the league's MVP award in 1987 and became known for drives late in games—forty to win and seven to tie.

The most famous came in the 1986 AFC title game at Cleveland, when he took the Broncos 98 yards in the final minutes to a tying TD, and they won in overtime.

"John Elway lifted that team on his back and took them to the Super Bowl," said Browns coach Marty Schottenheimer.[4]

JOHN ELWAY

BORN: June 28, 1960, Port Angeles, Washington.

. . . .

HIGH SCHOOL: Granada Hills High School, Granada Hills, California.

. . . .

COLLEGE: Stanford University.

. . . .

PRO CAREER: Denver Broncos, 1983–1998.

. . . .

RECORDS: Led Denver to record 47 fourth-quarter comebacks.

. . . .

HONORS: Pro Football Hall of Fame (2004); NFL Most Valuable Player (1987); Most Valuable Player, Super Bowl XXXIII.

. . . .

BRETT FAVRE

BRETT
FAVRE

Has anyone ever enjoyed playing football as much as Brett Favre?

Fans will remember the long completions in big games, or how his rocket arm could fire a pass between two defenders and right into his receiver's hands. Many of those receivers would admit that if they weren't paying attention, Favre's fastballs could break their fingers.

Fans also will remember Favre throwing snowballs at teammates during a 2007 playoff win over Seattle. Or how he carried receiver Greg Jennings on his shoulders after throwing the TD pass that broke Dan Marino's career record.

Or how about Favre sprinting downfield, his helmet off and a mile-long smile on his face after hitting Andre Rison for the first TD of his Super Bowl win in 1997?

"Everything we like about football is what Brett Favre is all about," said former NFL defensive lineman Tim Ryan.[1]

Favre was also about dealing with pain on and off the field. During his career, his wife Deanna fought breast cancer, and both her brother and stepfather died. So did Brett's dad, Irvin, who taught him everything about football back in the small town of Kiln, Mississippi.

"As professional athletes . . . sometimes people think we're bulletproof," Favre said. "But things like what have happened to me and my family really hit home."[2]

Irvin died in a car accident in December 2003. The next day, the Packers had a Monday night game at Oakland. Would Brett play?

Of course. Not only did Brett show up that night, he threw for 399 yards and four touchdowns before a national television audience.

"I knew that my dad would have wanted me to play," Favre said. "I love him so much, and I love this game. It's meant a great deal to me, to my dad. . . . I know he was watching tonight."[3]

Watching Favre was a pleasure, from the joy he showed for the game to the way he'd take risks and usually come out on top. Because he was always there.

"I saw Brett show up at the stadium on crutches," recalled former teammate Aaron Taylor, "then play in the game, throw a few touchdowns, and leave the stadium on crutches. He was the toughest man I ever played with."[4]

BRETT FAVRE

BORN: October 10, 1969, Gulfport, Mississippi.

HIGH SCHOOL: Hancock North Central High School, Pass Christian, Mississippi.

COLLEGE: University of Southern Mississippi.

PRO CAREER: Atlanta Falcons, 1991; Green Bay Packers, 1992–2007; New York Jets, 2008; Minnesota Vikings, 2009–present.

RECORDS: NFL Career Completions, Attempts, Touchdown Passes, Interceptions, and Yards Passing.

HONORS: NFL Most Valuable Player (1995, '96, '97); Selected for 10 Pro Bowls

OTTO GRAHAM

OTTO
GRAHAM

They called him "Automatic Otto" for many reasons. For one, Otto Graham never missed a game as a professional. For another, his Cleveland Browns always had winning records.

And most incredibly, in his ten seasons leading the team in the All-America Football Conference and then the NFL, Graham took the Browns to the championship game every year.

Every year!

"The test of a quarterback is where his team finishes," said Paul Brown, Graham's coach in Cleveland. "By that standard, Otto Graham was the best of all time."[1]

Graham was 105–17–4 in regular-season games and 8–3 in the postseason. Even when the Browns moved into the NFL, supposedly a far better league than the AAFC, he never slowed. When he passed for four touchdowns in a 30–28 championship game upset of the Rams—Graham took Cleveland on drives of 65 yards to tie it and 57 yards to Lou Groza's winning field goal with 28 seconds left—Automatic Otto was the king of football.

"I liked all his quarterback skills," said Sammy Baugh, another all-time great passer. "I thought he was one of the better quarterbacks in the league. He had a smart head and a good arm."[2]

But Graham didn't think he was made to be a quarterback. He went to Northwestern University on a basketball scholarship and played intramural football—winning a championship, of course.

Soon afterward, the Northwestern coach asked him to try out for the varsity. All Otto did was become the starter, then an All-American quarterback. He also was an All-American in basketball.

When Graham headed to the pros, he joined the Browns in the AAFC rather than going to the NFL. He was the league's most valuable player three times, but the truest test of his skills came when the Browns became part of the NFL.

For its first game, Cleveland was matched with the NFL champion Eagles, who most NFL owners and players believed would embarrass the newcomers.

Otto Graham wouldn't allow that. His first NFL pass went for a touchdown, and the Browns routed the Eagles 35–10. It was the beginning of a half-decade of NFL excellence for Graham and the Browns.

After Graham retired, he became athletic director and football coach at the U.S. Coast Guard Academy before coaching the Washington Redskins for three seasons. In 1965, he was inducted into the Pro Football Hall of Fame.

OTTO GRAHAM

BORN: December 6, 1921, Waukegan, Illinois.

HIGH SCHOOL: Waukegan (Illinois) High School.

COLLEGE: Northwestern University.

PRO CAREER: Cleveland Browns (AAFC/NFL), 1946–1955.

RECORDS: Leading Passer in AAFC Four Times & the NFL Twice; Won 10 Division or League Championships in ten years.

HONORS: Pro Football Hall of Fame (1965); All-League Nine Times.

PEYTON MANNING

PEYTON
MANNING

Peyton Manning couldn't have been less happy. His Indianapolis Colts had just lost to Pittsburgh in a playoff game. Once again, Manning couldn't get the Colts to the Super Bowl.

On a rainy Miami night just over a year later, Manning's smile couldn't have been brighter. Sure, he was soaking wet, but he also was holding up the Vince Lombardi Trophy.

While Peyton has been among the NFL top quarterbacks throughout the decade and had a record-setting 2004 season considered one of the questions disappeared. At the end of that 29–17 win, in which Manning was Super Bowl MVP, no one could doubt his greatness.

"He's done it, he's gotten it behind him," Colts coach Tony Dungy said after that win. "I don't think there's anything you can say now, other than this guy is a Hall of Fame player and one of the greatest players to ever play the game."[1]

Mannings are born to be quarterbacks. Peyton's father, Archie, was one of the best in college football, but played on weak teams in the pros and never made the playoffs. Peyton's younger brother Eli was the first overall pick in the NFL draft in 2004, six years after Peyton was No. 1, and won a Super Bowl with the Giants a year after Peyton did it with the Colts.

In an era when most plays are chosen by coaches from the sideline, Peyton Manning has called nearly all of Indy's plays. He often comes to the line, sees how the defense is set, hand-signals to his teammates what he wants them to do, and yells out a play call. Almost always, he picks the right play.

"I think you have to be confident in your offense," Peyton said. "That's part of playing in the NFL, and the reason you have confidence is because of how hard you worked and how hard you prepared."[2]

Manning's pleasant personality has won him fans throughout football—and beyond. He even hosted NBC's *Saturday Night Live* in 2007, and was a hit with his goofiness. That also led to dozens of TV commercials starring Manning. "The guy's just plain funny," said teammate Reggie Wayne.[3]

A starter since the day he joined the Colts, he could hold most career passing records by the time he finishes his career. Not that records are on his mind. "Those are nice for the fans and the organization," Peyton said, "but they're nothing like winning a championship."[4]

PEYTON MANNING

BORN: March 24, 1976, New Orleans, Louisiana.

HIGH SCHOOL: Isidore Newman High School, New Orleans, Louisiana.

COLLEGE: University of Tennessee.

PRO CAREER: Indianapolis Colts, 1998–present.

RECORDS: NFL Completions (3,468), Yards Passing (41,626) and Touchdown Passes (306) in first ten seasons.

HONORS: NFL Most Valuable Player (2003, '04. '08); Most Valuable Player, Super Bowl XLI.

DAN MARINO

DAN
MARINO

Just one more time, Dan Marino
wanted to fire a pass over the
middle and have his favorite
receiver, Mark Clayton, catch it.

So Marino stood on the stage after making his
induction speech at the Pro Football Hall of
Fame, and let fly a final perfect spiral to Clayton in the audience as the crowd cheered.

"Of course, in the end, every quarterback

passing leader in nearly all areas: touchdowns (420), yards (61,361 yards, or nearly 35 miles), completions (4,967). In all, he held 21 NFL marks when he retired from the Miami Dolphins in 2000.

In 1984, his second pro season, Marino shattered the record for TD passes with 48, a mark since broken by Peyton Manning, then Tom Brady. He guided the Dolphins into the Super Bowl, where they lost to another all-time great QB, Joe Montana, and the 49ers.

Oddly, that would be the only Super Bowl appearance for Marino. Even though he was the NFL's best passer for more than a decade, the Dolphins either had a weak defense or no running game to help him go deep in the playoffs. Still, Marino is remembered for his rocket arm, his smarts, his competitiveness, and his leadership.

"One of the things that made Dan so successful was the way he took charge," said Don Shula, head coach for nearly all of Marino's career. "In the locker room, the huddle, on the bench, you always knew who was in charge."[2]

One time Marino wasn't in charge was during the 1983 draft. Five other college passers—including future Hall of Famers John Elway and Jim Kelly—were chosen ahead of him.

When Miami's turn came at No. 27, the choice was easy: No. 13 from Pitt, quarterback Dan Marino. For the next seventeen seasons, beginning with a brilliant rookie year, Marino made Miami proud.

"When Danny came in his rookie year and set the world on fire, he set the bar awful high for the rest of us in the class," Elway said. "From that point on, we were all chasing Danny."[3]

They kept chasing Marino throughout his career, during which Dan also became a spokesman/fundraiser for several causes, including autism. His son Michael suffers from the disease.

DAN MARINO

BORN: September 15, 1961, Pittsburgh, Pennsylvania.

HIGH SCHOOL: Central Catholic High School, Pittsburgh, Pennsylvania.

COLLEGE: University of Pittsburgh.

PRO: Miami Dolphins, 1983–1999.

RECORDS: NFL's leading passer (upon retirement) with 4,967 completions, 8,358 attempts, 61,361 yards, 420 touchdowns; first to pass for 5,000 yards in a season.

HONORS: NFL Most Valuable Player, 1984; Pro Football Hall of Fame, 2005.

JOE MONTANA

JOE
MONTANA

Whether it was at Notre Dame or with the San Francisco 49ers, the team he guided to four Super Bowl championships, Joe Montana never lost his cool.

"Joe was so focused that you couldn't tell the difference with Joe between the first play in a game and when the next play could win the game," said former teammate Randy Cross. "He never got shaken and we just knew he'd do whatever it took."[1]

Maybe it was when he overcame chills, fever, and harsh, cold winds to bring Notre Dame back from a 34–12 hole and past Houston 35–34 in the 1979 Cotton Bowl. At halftime, team doctor Les Bodnar fed Montana some instant chicken soup. Then Joe Cool guided the big comeback.

Or perhaps it was how, in the final minutes of the 1989 Super Bowl, Montana stood in the 49ers' huddle, scanned the crowd and said: "Look, there's John Candy." After spotting the actor in the stands, Montana took San Francisco 92 yards to the winning touchdown, hitting eight of his nine passes, including a 10-yard TD strike to John Taylor with 34 seconds left.

"That drive was something I had done many times in my back yard," he said. "You accomplish a lot of things in your back yard. I won a bunch of Super Bowls by the time I was nine."[2]

Montana wasn't known for his powerful arm or his scrambling skills. It was his brain and his poise that made him stand out in an era of great quarterbacks and earned him two NFL MVP awards.

"I tried to be the same person all the time," Montana said. "Nerves are good. I wanted to be nervous."[3]

He was at his best in the biggest games. He never was intercepted in a Super Bowl (in 122 attempts) and had six 300-yard passing games in the postseason. When Montana retired in 1995, he ranked second in career passer rating (92.3) and was 4–0 in Super Bowls.

Yet he was only a third-round draft pick in 1979, when 49ers coach Bill Walsh saw Montana as a good fit for the West Coast offense Walsh had designed. Through all his success, Joe Cool had fun.

"Nothing comes close to a Sunday afternoon, the ups and downs," he said. "This is a game that gets to you in a special way."[4]

JOE MONTANA

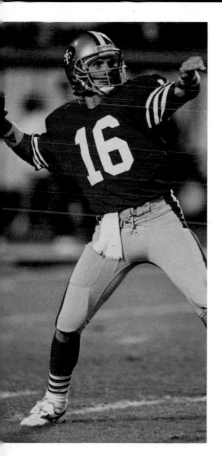

BORN: June 11, 1956, Monongahela, Pennsylvania.

HIGH SCHOOL: Ringgold High School, Monongahela, Pennsylvania.

COLLEGE: University of Notre Dame.

PRO CAREER: San Francisco 49ers, 1979–1992; Kansas City Chiefs, 1993–94.

RECORDS: NFL Most Consecutive Passes Completed (22); NFL Highest Passer Rating (at retirement, 93.5).

HONORS: Pro Football Hall of Fame (2000); NFL Most Valuable Player, 1989–90; Most Valuable Player, Super Bowls XVI, XIX, XXIV.

JOHNNY UNITAS

JOHNNY
UNITAS

With his black high-tops, crew cut, and hunched shoulders, John Unitas didn't look the part of star quarterback. Then he threw the football, and everyone knew they were watching greatness.

Unitas broke nearly every NFL passing record in an eighteen-year career that ended in 1973. He won three championships with the Baltimore Colts in the pre-Super Bowl days, and is credited for modernizing pro football offenses defenses were doing, and his passing ability changed the game. "His presence in Baltimore and in the history of the NFL is unmatched," said former Baltimore Ravens coach Brian Billick.[1]

Unitas was drafted in the ninth round in 1955 out of the University of Louisville by the Pittsburgh Steelers, who then cut him. He hitchhiked home, unsure if he'd get another chance at pro football. He did when the Colts signed him the next year.

"Unitas was signed after we received a letter from a fan telling us there was a player in Bloomfield deserving a chance," then Colts coach Weeb Ewbank said a few years later. "I always accused Johnny of writing it."[2]

By 1958 the Colts were playing for the NFL championship against the Giants at Yankee Stadium. That game, the first nationally televised, was Unitas' most famous performance.

New York led by three points with one and a half minutes remaining. Johnny U completed four passes to set up a tying field goal. For the first time, an NFL championship game went to overtime.

"The first playoff ever to go to sudden death . . . you can't have much more drama than that," Unitas said after taking the Colts on an 80-yard drive to the winning touchdown.[3]

Baltimore would win the NFL crown in 1959 and 1968. In 1964 and '67, Unitas was the league's Most Valuable Player, and he was chosen 1960s Player of the Decade.

In all, Unitas went to ten Pro Bowls. He once threw a TD pass in 47 consecutive games. He retired after one season (1973) with the San Diego Chargers.

"He was the first of the great modern quarterbacks, and his performance set the standard for everyone who followed him at that position," said Don Shula, pro football's winningest coach.[4]

JOHNNY UNITAS

BORN: May 7, 1933, Pittsburgh, Pennsylvania.

. . . .

HIGH SCHOOL: St Justin's High School, Pittsburgh, Pennsylvania.

. . . .

COLLEGE: University of Louisville.

. . . .

PRO CAREER: Baltimore Colts, 1956–1972; San Diego Chargers, 1973.

. . . .

RECORDS: Led Colts to 1958, 1959 NFL Championships, Super Bowl V Victory; Consecutive Games with TD Pass (47).

. . . .

HONORS: NFL Most Valuable Player, 1964, 1967; Pro Football Hall of Fame, 1979.

. . . .

CHAPTER 1. SAMMY BAUGH

1. Associated Press, August 22, 2002.
2. Ibid.

CHAPTER 2. TERRY BRADSHAW

1. Associated Press, Pro Football Hall of Fame, August 7, 1989.
2. Ibid.
3. Associated Press, July 29, 1989.

CHAPTER 3. TOM BRADY

1. Author interview, January 6, 2008.
2. Associated Press, January 9, 2008.
3. Author interview, February 1, 2003.
4. Associated Press, December 22, 2007.

CHAPTER 4. JOHN ELWAY

1. Author interview, August 9, 2004.
2. Author interview, January 27, 1998.
3. Associated Press, September 14, 1999.
4. Author interview, January 12, 1987.

CHAPTER 5. BRETT FAVRE

1. Sirius NFL Radio, March 4, 2008.
2. Associated Press, August 23, 2007.
3. "Favre Honors His Father With Spectacular Effort," *Oakland Tribune*, December 23, 2003, <http://findarticles.com/p/articles/mi_qn4176/is_20031223/ai_n14560367/> (September 18, 2009).
4. Sirius NFL Radio, March 4, 2008.

CHAPTER 6. OTTO GRAHAM

1. Associated Press, December 18, 2003.
2. Ibid.

CHAPTER 7. PEYTON MANNING

1. "Finally! Manning Reaches Pinacle With Win," *NFL.com*, February 4, 2007, <http://www.indystar.com/apps/pbcs.dll/article?AID=/20070205/> (September 18, 2009).
2. Author interview, February 1, 2007.
3. Author interview, March 27, 2007.
4. Author interview, February 3, 2007.

Chapter 8. Dan MARINO

1. Associated Press, Pro Football Hall of Fame, August 7, 2005.
2. Author interview, February 5, 2005.
3. "Dan Marino Brings Down the House in Tribute," *Miami Herald*, August 24, 2000, <http://www.accessmylibrary.com/coms2/summary_0286-7281781_ITM> (September 18, 2009).

Chapter 9. Joe MONTANA

1. Author interview, July 31, 1990.
2. Associated Press, January 29, 2000.
3. Associated Press, Pro Football Hall of Fame, July 27, 2000.
4. Ibid.

Chapter 10. Johnny UNITAS

1. Associated Press, September 12, 2002.
2. Ibid.
3. "Johnny Unitas," *Legacy.com*, September 12, 2002, <http://www.legacy.com/Obituaries.asp?page=lifestory&personid=485764> (September 18, 2009).
4. Associated Press, Sept. 12, 2002.

Further Reading

Stewart, Mark and Mike Kennedy. *Touchdown: The Power and Precision of Football's Perfect Play.* Minneapolis, Minn.: Millbrook Press, 2010.

Sullivan, George. *Quarterbacks!: Eighteen of Football's Greatest.* New York: Atheneum, 1998.

Internet Addresses

The Official Site of the National Football League
http://www.nfl.com

Pro Football Hall of Fame
http://www.profootballhof.com